Reading Links

1

Andrew E. Bennett

NAN'UN-DO

Reading Links 1

Written and designed by: Andrew E. Bennett

Reading Links 1
Image Credits

Shutterstock: p. 8 (©Shutterstock);
iStock Photos: pp. 10, 12, 16, 18, 20, 22, 26 (baby tiger), 30 (bottom left, bottom right (top right, bottom), 32, 34, 36, 38, 46 (right), 48, 56, 60, 62, 64, 68 (left), 72, 76, 80, 84 (© iStock Photos);
Corel: p. 14 (© Corel);
DJ Soft: p. 24 (© Dance & Jump Software);
Hemera: pp. 26 (all but baby tiger), 30 (top left, top right, bottom right (top left), 78 (© Hemera);
Andrew E. Bennett: p. 28 (© Andrew E. Bennett);
Q Vision: p. 40 (© Q Vision Co.);
Grace Kuo: p. 42 (© Andrew E. Bennett);
Dainippon: p. 44 (© Dainippon Screen MFG Co.);
Idea Design Center: p. 46 (left) (© Idea Design Center);
Xiao Peng: p. 50 (© Andrew E. Bennett);
Sam: p. 52 (© Andrew E. Bennett);
Mixa: p. 54 (© Dainippon Screen MFG Co.);
D Cube Computer Studio: p. 68 (right) (© D Cube Computer Studio);
Image DJ: p. 82 (© Image DJ Corp)

Contents

Download Audio

音声ファイル
無料 DL
のご案内

このテキストの音声を無料で視聴（ストリーミング）・ダウンロードできます。自習用音声としてご活用ください。
以下のサイトにアクセスしてテキスト番号で検索してください。

https://nanun-do.com　テキスト番号［ **512089** ］

※ 無線 LAN（WiFi）に接続してのご利用を推奨いたします。

※ 音声ダウンロードは Zip ファイルでの提供になります。
お使いの機器によっては別途ソフトウェア（アプリケーション）の導入が必要となります。

Read by

Rachel Walzer
Chris Koprowski

※ Reading Links 1 音声ダウンロードページは
以下の QR コードからもご利用になれます。

Introduction

Reading Links is a comprehensive series designed for lower-level students. Each book includes 20 units centered on high-interest topics such as the arts, careers, entertainment, the environment, and many others.

Reading passages and exercises use carefully controlled vocabulary and grammar to facilitate comprehension. Critical thinking and active student engagement are also encouraged. Unit after unit, students' reading, vocabulary, grammar, listening, and speaking skills are strengthened.

Following is an explanation of the unit components:

The general topic is given next to the unit number.

Units are divided into two parts covering different aspects of the topic. Part 1 starts with a story or article. In *Reading Links 1*, these passages are between 50-75 words long. Sentences are on average less than 10 words long. The track number next to the headphones icon corresponds to the downloadable audio recording of the passage.

This vocabulary building exercise contains four target words or phrases selected from the reading passage. They are chosen for their frequency and usefulness. To build fluency further, students can be asked to write their own sentences using the target words.

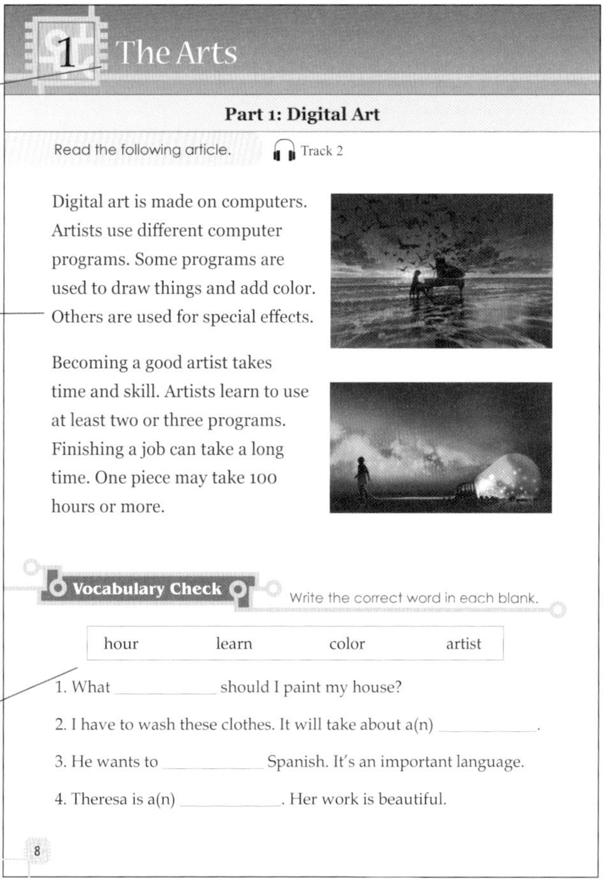

1 The Arts

Part 1: Digital Art

Read the following article. Track 2

Digital art is made on computers. Artists use different computer programs. Some programs are used to draw things and add color. Others are used for special effects.

Becoming a good artist takes time and skill. Artists learn to use at least two or three programs. Finishing a job can take a long time. One piece may take 100 hours or more.

Vocabulary Check Write the correct word in each blank.

hour	learn	color	artist

1. What __________ should I paint my house?
2. I have to wash these clothes. It will take about a(n) __________.
3. He wants to __________ Spanish. It's an important language.
4. Theresa is a(n) __________. Her work is beautiful.

8

Reading Check Choose the best answer.

1. ( ) Digital artists __________.
   A: all use the same programs
   B: rarely use computers
   C: need to have skill
   D: usually finish jobs quickly
2. ( ) What does the article say about computer programs?
   A: They can be expensive.
   B: They take two or three hours to learn.
   C: They are only used for adding color.
   D: They have different uses.
3. ( ) How can you become a digital artist?
   A: Draw a lot with a pen and paper.
   B: Work hard to learn computer programs.
   C: Spend 100 hours reading about art.
   D: Find a person with time and skill.
4. ( ) In the second paragraph, what is a "job"?
   A: a piece of digital art
   B: a computer art class
   C: a period of time
   D: a way to meet artists

Grammar Check Write the correct form of each word.

Ex: We enjoy *looking* (look) at art.

1. I like __________ (use) computers.
2. __________ (Learn) to paint takes time.
3. This program is good for __________ (make) movies.
4. My sister is good at __________ (tell) stories.

9

This reading comprehension exercise includes detail, analysis, and vocabulary questions. Some questions go beneath the surface, encouraging students to consider the material more deeply and employ critical thinking skills.

Each grammar check covers an important language structure such as pronouns, word forms, verb tenses, prepositions, and so on. There are also several word order exercises in which students rearrange words to make a complete sentence.

Part 2 opens with a unique element of *Reading Links*: a visual reading component. It is included because in today's world, literacy extends beyond the ability to read passages of text. It means being able to read maps, graphs, tables, charts, schedules, dialogues, and so on.

In *Reading Links*, these components are presented in simplified, yet authentic English to provide students an opportunity to practice and improve these critical 21st century skills.

Part 2: Event Schedule

Look at the following information.

What to do in New York: May 12-18

Shows	Music
Chicago Tickets: $25 - $150 Time: Daily. 8:00 PM	**Jazz** Location: The Music Well Time: Starts at 6:00 PM
Phantom of the Opera Tickets: $35 - $175 Time: Mon, Wed. 8:00 PM	**Rock** Location: Rock the Clock Time: Starts at 7:30 PM

Museums	Free Events
Museum of Modern Art Special showing: French art Open: 10:00 AM - 6:00 PM	**Music in the park** Location: Central Park Date: May 17 (all day)
Metropolitan Museum Special showing: Glass art Open: 10:00 AM - 7:00 PM	**Walking tour of New York** Location: Starts at Lincoln Center Date: May 18. 2:00 PM

True or False Circle true (T) or false (F).

1. (T/F) Some activities don't cost any money.
2. (T/F) The Museum of Modern Art has a music event.
3. (T/F) Every listing tells you the nearest subway station.
4. (T/F) On Monday, you can see *Chicago* or *Phantom of the Opera*.

10

This basic true and false exercise checks students' understanding of the material. Teachers are encouraged to go further and base classroom activities on the visual reading components through role plays, student-generated materials and presentations, etc.

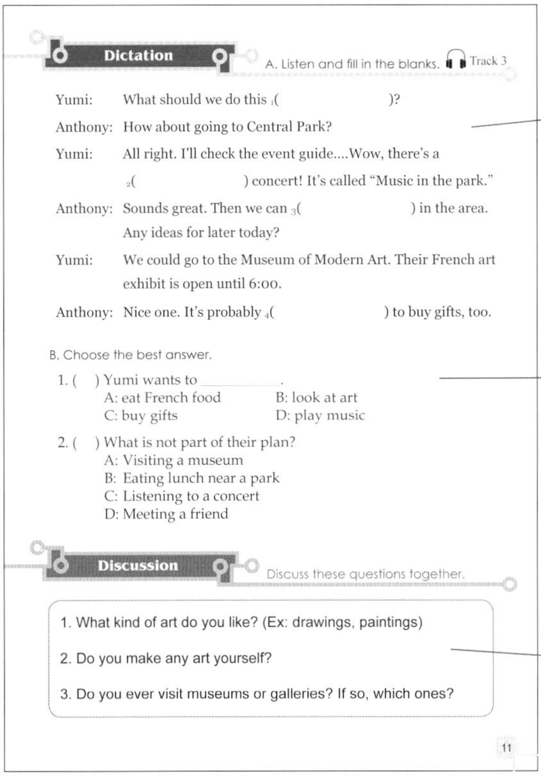
Dictation A. Listen and fill in the blanks. Track 3

Yumi: What should we do this 1(   )?

Anthony: How about going to Central Park?

Yumi: All right. I'll check the event guide....Wow, there's a 2(   ) concert! It's called "Music in the park."

Anthony: Sounds great. Then we can 3(   ) in the area. Any ideas for later today?

Yumi: We could go to the Museum of Modern Art. Their French art exhibit is open until 6:00.

Anthony: Nice one. It's probably 4(   ) to buy gifts, too.

B. Choose the best answer.

1. (   ) Yumi wants to ________.
   A: eat French food   B: look at art
   C: buy gifts   D: play music

2. (   ) What is not part of their plan?
   A: Visiting a museum
   B: Eating lunch near a park
   C: Listening to a concert
   D: Meeting a friend

Discussion Discuss these questions together.

1. What kind of art do you like? (Ex: drawings, paintings)
2. Do you make any art yourself?
3. Do you ever visit museums or galleries? If so, which ones?

11

This dialogue is related to the unit's general topic. The track number next to the headphones icon corresponds to the downloadable audio recording of the dialogue. Students should listen to the audio recording and fill in the blanks. As a fluency building exercise, students can then pair up and take turns reading each character's lines.

The dialogue is followed by a comprehension exercise.

Finally, there is a series of discussion questions related to Part 1 and Part 2 of the unit. Students may ask each other questions in pairs, or the class can answer the questions together. Students are encouraged to go beyond "yes/no" answers and provide examples and details from their own lives, as well as reasons for their points of view.

Additional materials for *Reading Links 1* are available. They include downloadable MP3 files of the audio recordings, which make it easy for students to listen to the recordings on their computer, phone, or other device.

The book's teacher's manual includes the full listening transcript, answer key, and other resources.

Materials to assist with online classes are also available from Nan'un-do.

I hope *Reading Links 1* helps build students' English skills while boosting everyone's interest and confidence in an enjoyable way.

Thank you very much, and best wishes for an outstanding class!

Andrew E. Bennett

1 The Arts

Part 1: Digital Art

Read the following article. Track 2

Digital art is made on computers. Artists use different computer programs. Some programs are used to draw things and add color. Others are used for special effects.

Becoming a good artist takes time and skill. Artists learn to use at least two or three programs. Finishing a job can take a long time. One piece may take 100 hours or more.

Vocabulary Check

Write the correct word in each blank.

hour	learn	color	artist

1. What ____________ should I paint my house?

2. I have to wash these clothes. It will take about a(n) ____________.

3. He wants to ____________ Spanish. It's an important language.

4. Theresa is a(n) ____________. Her work is beautiful.

Reading Check

Choose the best answer.

1. (   ) Digital artists ___________.
   A: all use the same programs
   B: rarely use computers
   C: need to have skill
   D: usually finish jobs quickly

2. (   ) What does the article say about computer programs?
   A: They can be expensive.
   B: They take two or three hours to learn.
   C: They are only used for adding color.
   D: They have different uses.

3. (   ) How can you become a digital artist?
   A: Draw a lot with a pen and paper.
   B: Work hard to learn computer programs.
   C: Spend 100 hours reading about art.
   D: Find a person with time and skill.

4. (   ) In the second paragraph, what is a "job"?
   A: a piece of digital art
   B: a computer art class
   C: a period of time
   D: a way to meet artists

Grammar Check

Write the correct form of each word.

Ex: We enjoy _*looking*_ (look) at art.

1. I like ___________ (use) computers.

2. ___________ (Learn) to paint takes time.

3. This program is good for ___________ (make) movies.

4. My sister is good at ___________ (tell) stories.

Part 2: Event Schedule

Look at the following information.

What to do in New York: May 12-18

Shows

Chicago
Tickets: $25 - $150
Time: Daily. 8:00 PM

Phantom of the Opera
Tickets: $35 - $175
Time: Mon, Wed. 8:00 PM

Music

Jazz
Location: The Music Well
Time: Starts at 6:00 PM

Rock
Location: Rock the Clock
Time: Starts at 7:30 PM

Museums

Museum of Modern Art
Special showing: French art
Open: 10:00 AM - 6:00 PM

Metropolitan Museum
Special showing: Glass art
Open: 10:00 AM - 7:00 PM

Free Events

Music in the park
Location: Central Park
Date: May 17 (all day)

Walking tour of New York
Location: Starts at Lincoln Center
Date: May 18. 2:00 PM

True or False

Circle true (T) or false (F).

1. (T/F) Some activities don't cost any money.
2. (T/F) The Museum of Modern Art has a music event.
3. (T/F) Every listing tells you the nearest subway station.
4. (T/F) On Monday, you can see *Chicago* or *Phantom of the Opera.*

Dictation

A. Listen and fill in the blanks. Track 3

Yumi: What should we do this $_1$( )?

Anthony: How about going to Central Park?

Yumi: All right. I'll check the event guide.... Wow, there's a $_2$( ) concert! It's called "Music in the park."

Anthony: Sounds great. Then we can $_3$( ) in the area. Any ideas for later today?

Yumi: We could go to the Museum of Modern Art. Their French art exhibit is open until 6:00.

Anthony: Nice one. It's probably $_4$( ) to buy gifts, too.

B. Choose the best answer.

1. ( ) Yumi wants to ___________.
   A: eat French food B: look at art
   C: buy gifts D: play music

2. ( ) What is not part of their plan?
   A: Visiting a museum
   B: Eating lunch near a park
   C: Listening to a concert
   D: Meeting a friend

Discussion

Discuss these questions together.

1. What kind of art do you like? (Ex: drawings, paintings)
2. Do you make any art yourself?
3. Do you ever visit museums or galleries? If so, which ones?

2 Incredible Races

Part 1: The Iditarod

Read the following article. Track 4

The Iditarod is a dogsled race across Alaska. Every March, around 65 teams take part. Each team includes one person and up to 16 dogs.

Together, they race almost 2,000 kilometers. It's a long, hard, and very cold race. Just finishing the Iditarod is a challenge. Winning it is a dream come true.

Vocabulary Check

Write the correct word in each blank.

almost	dream	hard	across

1. My ______________ is to open my own pet store.

2. The truck is ______________ full. There's room for one more box.

3. Sam's job is ______________. He works 12 hours a day.

4. Katie, my classmate, lives ______________ the street.

Reading Check

Choose the best answer.

1. (   ) About how many teams race in the Iditarod?
   A: 16
   B: 17
   C: 65
   D: 2,000

2. (   ) The article does not say the race is ___________.
   A: short
   B: hard
   C: long
   D: cold

3. (   ) "Winning it is a dream come true." What does this mean?
   A: All of the stories about the Iditarod are true.
   B: Everything in life is a challenge.
   C: People think about winning it for a long time.
   D: Most people dream at night.

4. (   ) What does the article suggest about the Iditarod?
   A: The length of the race changes yearly.
   B: Teams have to work hard just to finish.
   C: Every team has a good chance of winning.
   D: Racers only win in their dreams.

Grammar Check

Complete each sentence with *it*, *its*, or *it's*.

Ex: ___*It's*___ getting dark outside.

1. A dog and ___________ owner are good friends.

2. ___________ time to go home.

3. I'm curious about the note. What does ___________ say?

4. I love ___________ here. The food is amazing.

Part 2: Weather and the Iditarod

Look at the following weather report.

Anchorage is the starting point of the Iditarod. Ophir is in the middle of the race. The finish line is in Nome. Here is a weather report for these three places.

	Currently (March 5)		Three-Day Forecast		
				Conditions	High/Low
Anchorage	1°	 Sunny	March 6		0°/-6°
			March 7		-2°/-8°
			March 8		-3°/-10°
				Conditions	High/Low
Ophir	-2°	 Cloudy	March 6		-3°/-8°
			March 7		-5°/-10°
			March 8		-6°/-11°
				Conditions	High/Low
Nome	-8°	 Snowy	March 6		-9°/-15°
			March 7		-10°/-17°
			March 8		-11°/-19°

True or False

Circle true (T) or false (F).

1. (T/F) Currently, it is cloudy in Ophir.

2. (T/F) Anchorage may see a low of -8° on March 7.

3. (T/F) Ophir will be colder than Nome on March 6.

4. (T/F) On March 8, all three places expect snow.

Dictation

A. Listen and fill in the blanks. Track 5

Kiki: The marathon is this 1(   ). It will pass right in front of our building.

Matt: Should we watch it from the 2(   )?

Kiki: Actually, I want to stand outside. It's such a long race. I have 30 3(   ) for the racers.

Matt: You're always so nice to people. Do you want some help?

Kiki: That would be great. The water is a 4(   ).

Matt: No problem. I'll bring it downstairs.

B. Choose the best answer.

1. (   ) Matt offers to ________.
   A: buy some water   B: carry something heavy
   C: run in the race   D: clean the window

2. (   ) What do we learn about the marathon?
   A: The whole race is in another city.
   B: It takes place during the weekend.
   C: It might rain in the morning.
   D: You can't give things to runners.

Discussion

Discuss these questions together.

1. Do you ever watch long races? (Ex: the Iditarod, marathons, long-distance skiing)
2. What does it take to become a good racer? (Ex: training)
3. Would you ever join a long-distance race? Why or why not?

3 Movies

Part 1: Movie Snacks

Read the following article. Track 6

Snacks and movies go hand in hand. Popcorn is the most famous movie snack. Some people eat it plain. Others like it sweet or salty. You can also put butter on top.

Candy and chocolate are two other popular snacks. Movie theaters also sell drinks like soda and tea. Going to the movies is a lot of fun. Snacks make the day out even better.

Vocabulary Check

Write the correct word in each blank.

movie	fun	eat	famous

1. The actor is really ______________. Everyone knows him.
2. I'm going to see a(n) ______________ after work.
3. What do you want to ______________ for lunch?
4. Did you have ______________ at the park?

Reading Check

Choose the best answer.

1. (   ) What does the article say about popcorn?
   A: People enjoy different flavors.
   B: Everyone likes it the same way.
   C: Only a few theaters sell it.
   D: It's better to eat popcorn salty.

2. (   ) Which movie snack is not discussed in the article?
   A: Chocolate
   B: Popcorn
   C: Potato chips
   D: Candy

3. (   ) What does "go hand in hand" mean?
   A: be easy to carry
   B: go together well
   C: have a fun time
   D: be very friendly

4. (   ) What does the article say about movie theaters?
   A: It's better to see movies at night.
   B: Some theaters give you free popcorn.
   C: Just a few let you eat snacks inside.
   D: Besides snacks, they also sell drinks.

Grammar Check

Complete each sentence with *few*, *many*, or *lot*.

Ex: There are just a ___*few*___ people in line.

1. Do you have a __________ minutes? I'd like to ask you something.

2. My computer has a __________ of problems. I need a new one.

3. __________ people are here for the concert. Every seat is full.

4. The sports car has a __________ of power.

Part 2: Movie Posters

Look at these movie posters.

True or False

Circle true (T) or false (F).

1. (T/F) In Japan, *Electric Kid* might open in July.

2. (T/F) Each poster shows the director's name.

3. (T/F) Chad Thurman is probably older than Blake Strong.

4. (T/F) The Craftsmen wrote the music for *Across the Golden Gate*.

Dictation

A. Listen and fill in the blanks. Track 7

Dorian: What movie should we see?

Cheryl: Something light – no horror films or 1( ) that. How about a comedy?

Dorian: That could work. Let's see something with 2( ). Romantic comedies aren't really my thing.

Cheryl: I hear you.... All right, I found the movie listings. We have a couple of good 3( ). Actually, one is a cartoon.

Dorian: That 4( ). Should we check out the reviews and decide?

Cheryl: Let's do it.

B. Choose the best answer.

1. ( ) Dorian wants to see __________.
   A: a romantic movie B: any kind of cartoon
   C: an action comedy D: a horror film

2. ( ) What will they probably do next?
   A: Invite a friend somewhere
   B: Drive to the theater
   C: Read some movie reviews
   D: Buy popcorn

Discussion

Discuss these questions together.

1. What kinds of movies do you like?
2. What are your favorite movie snacks?
3. Do you like reading movie reviews? Do they affect your decisions about movies?

4 Careers

Part 1: The Knowledge

Read the following article. Track 8

London, England is a very big city. Becoming a taxi driver there is hard. First, people take a course called the "Knowledge." Finishing the Knowledge takes several years. You study 400 different routes. You also learn about London's famous places. Then you must pass some tests. Finally, you can become a London taxi driver.

Vocabulary Check

Write the correct word in each blank.

year	course	become	several

1. There are ____________ apples left. Would you like one?

2. To ____________ rich, you must work hard. A little luck also helps.

3. I want to travel to Kenya next ____________.

4. My graphic design ____________ is so good. The professor is great.

Reading Check

Choose the best answer.

1. (　　) What is the Knowledge?
   A: A course of study　　B: A place in London
   C: A famous school　　D: A group of cities

2. (　　) To become a London taxi driver, you do not ________.
   A: study many routes
   B: take more than one test
   C: learn the Knowledge
   D: teach people about taxis

3. (　　) What comes last?
   A: Learning about famous places
   B: Getting to know 400 routes
   C: Becoming a London taxi driver
   D: Studying the Knowledge

4. (　　) Which of these is true?
   A: Drivers can pay money to pass the Knowledge.
   B: Drivers learn about 4,000 different streets.
   C: There are around 400 London taxi drivers.
   D: Finishing the Knowledge takes more than one year.

Grammar Check

Complete each sentence with *first*, *then*, or *finally*.

Ex: It's going to be a great day. *First* , let's have breakfast.

Sundays are busy days for me. ________ (1), I have a piano lesson. That's in the morning. ________ (2) I have lunch with some friends. That's the fun part of the day. ________ (3) I take my dog for a walk. ________ (4), I clean my house. I sure work hard on the weekend!

Part 2: Interview with a Fire Fighter

Read the following conversation.

Linda: Tell me about fire fighting.

Mr. Jones: Well, it's very hot. It can be dangerous. So, you need a lot of training.

Linda: Is fighting fires your only job?

Mr. Jones: Actually, no. We also help in medical emergencies.

Linda: What do you like about being a fire fighter?

Mr. Jones: It's something I enjoy. Sure, it's hard. But I like helping others. It makes me feel good about myself.

True or False

Circle true (T) or false (F).

1. (T/F) The conversation's purpose is to train someone.
2. (T/F) Besides fighting fires, Mr. Jones helps injured people.
3. (T/F) Mr. Jones likes his work.
4. (T/F) Linda asks about fire fighters' equipment.

Dictation

A. Listen and fill in the blanks. Track 9

Ken: What's your 1(   ) after graduating?

Nora: I want to get a job in 2(   ). It's such a fast-growing field.

Ken: And an 3(   ) one. It's good work, and it's great for the planet.

Nora: Exactly. How about yourself?

Ken: I'm not sure yet. My major is architecture. I might 4(   ). But my passion is acting.

Nora: Both of those sound interesting.

B. Choose the best answer.

1. (   ) Ken ____________ Nora's idea.
   A: disagrees with   B: remembers
   C: doesn't understand   D: likes

2. (   ) Which of these is true?
   A: Ken is studying to be an actor.
   B: Nora doesn't have any future plans.
   C: The friends may work together.
   D: Ken has a big decision to make.

Discussion

Discuss these questions together.

1. Do you have any career plans?

2. Many people start their own businesses. Would that interest you?

3. Would you ever consider doing dangerous work? (Ex: being a fire fighter)

5 Animals

Part 1: Chimpanzees

Read the following article. Track 10

Chimpanzees are smart animals. They can solve many kinds of problems. They make and use tools. And they have good communication skills.

Chimps live in groups. There are from 2 to 80 animals in a group. During the day, they find food together. They like to eat fruits and leaves. At night, chimps sleep in trees.

Vocabulary Check

Write the correct word in each blank.

live	tool	group	problem

1. There are four people in our ____________.

2. It's a big ____________. Can you really solve it?

3. I want to ____________ in Prague. It's such an interesting city.

4. I'll use this ____________ to remove the bicycle tire.

Reading Check

Choose the best answer.

1. (   ) How do chimpanzees find food?
   A: They look for it together.
   B: They look for food at night in trees.
   C: They look for fruit with leaves on it.
   D: They look for food alone.

2. (   ) When might chimps look for food?
   A: At 2:00 AM
   B: At 11:00 AM
   C: At 8:00 PM
   D: At 11:00 PM

3. (   ) Chimps can solve many problems. What is this an example of?
   A: The way chimps find food
   B: The way chimps are smart
   C: The way chimps live in groups
   D: The way chimps like to sleep

4. (   ) Which of these is true about chimps?
   A: For chimps, learning to use tools is hard.
   B: Chimps only live in zoos these days.
   C: Some groups have fewer than 10 animals.
   D: They don't have a way to communicate.

Grammar Check

Put the words in the correct order.

1. (solved / problem / math / We / the)

   ____.

2. (a / works / brother / gym / at / My)

   ____.

3. (birds / There / here / many kinds / are / of)

   ____.

Part 2: Website

Look at the following website.

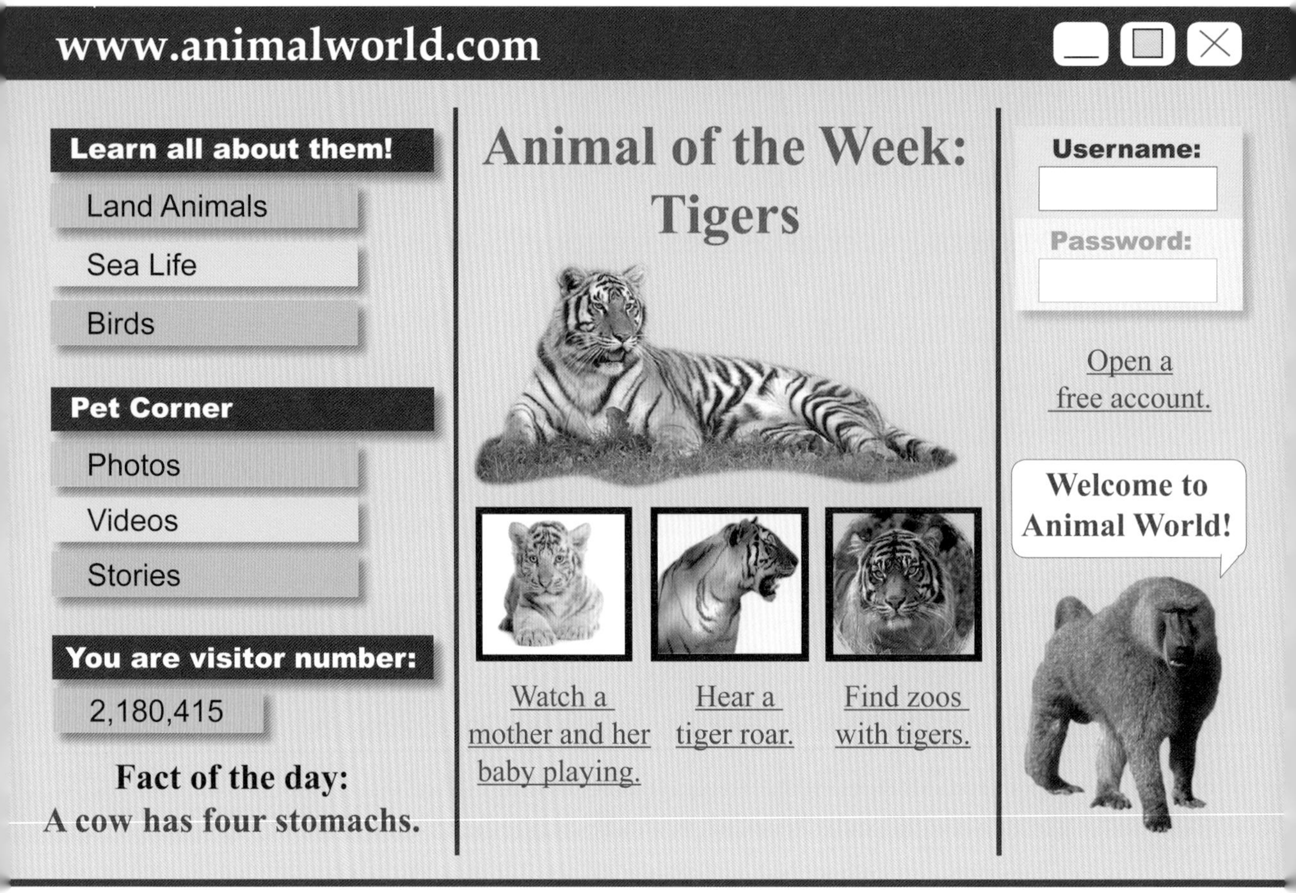

True or False

Circle true (T) or false (F).

1. (T/F) The visitor number is on the left side of the page.

2. (T/F) In the Animal of the Week section, you can read about cows.

3. (T/F) Signing up for an account is free.

4. (T/F) The website is only about land animals.

Dictation

A. Listen and fill in the blanks. Track 11

Felix: Seeing elephants 1(   ) is amazing. They're so big!

Dora: And smart. I wonder if they're 2(   ).

Felix: Good question. The zoo tries its best. The elephants have plenty of food.

Dora: That's true. Do you think they want to be free?

Felix: Maybe. I think the 3(   ) do. The lions and tigers sometimes look sad.

Dora: I know what you mean. Well, one thing's for sure. The monkeys always 4(   )!

B. Choose the best answer.

1. (   ) Dora thinks the ____________ are probably happy.
   A: monkeys   B: tigers
   C: elephants   D: lions

2. (   ) What does Felix say about the zoo?
   A: The elephants get enough food.
   B: The animals have plenty of room.
   C: The big cats always look sad.
   D: The monkeys love playing with tigers.

Discussion

Discuss these questions together.

1. Which animals are smart?

2. Which animals do you like seeing in zoos?

3. Do animals in zoos have good lives? Why or why not?

6 Handmade Items

Part 1: Glass Blowing

Read the following article. Track 12

We can make beautiful things with glass. One way is by glass blowing. The art form is 2,000 years old.

First, the artist heats the glass. Then, he or she blows air into it. That changes the shape. The artist turns, pushes, and pulls the hot glass. The shape changes more.

Finally, the work of art is done. It may be a cup, bowl, or something else. Often, the work is both useful and beautiful.

Vocabulary Check

Write the correct word in each blank.

beautiful	change	shape	turn

1. Look at the ______________ of this pillow. It looks like the moon.
2. I want to ______________ my hairstyle. My hair is too long.
3. The ring is ______________. I love the little blue stones.
4. To open the door, ______________ the key again.

Reading Check

Choose the best answer.

1. ( ) Glass works of art ________.
   A: are only for looking at
   B: last about 2,000 years
   C: are all the same size
   D: may be useful items

2. ( ) Why does the artist pull the glass?
   A: To heat it up
   B: To finish the work
   C: To change the shape
   D: To make a sound

3. ( ) Which of these is true?
   A: Glass blowing is a new art.
   B: The artist must not turn the glass.
   C: Bowls are harder to make than cups.
   D: Pushing the glass changes it.

4. ( ) For glass to change shape, it probably ________.
   A: needs to be hot   B: can be hot or cold
   C: must be a little cold   D: should be very cold

Grammar Check

Write the correct word in each blank.

Ex: I love this bag. It's so *useful*.
(useful / usefully)

1. We need to finish ________. The shop is about to close.
   (quick/quickly)

2. Your necklace is ________.
   (beautiful/beautifully)

3. The birds are singing ________.
   (happy/happily)

4. The ________ man is pulling a train!
   (strong/strongly)

Part 2: Building a Model

Read the following information.

Building a model is fun. Here is a basic guide.

1. First, choose a model to build. Cars, trains, boats, and airplanes are popular kinds.

2. Next, find a place to build your model. It should be a clean area.

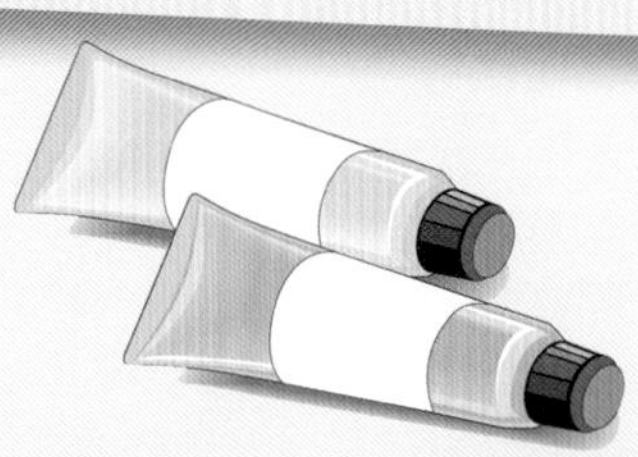

3. Then, read the instructions carefully. Use special glue to put the pieces together.

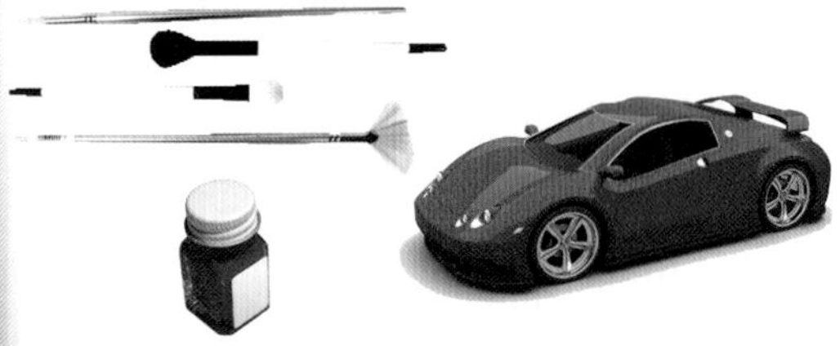

4. Finally, paint your model. Use any colors you like!

True or False

Circle true (T) or false (F).

1. (T/F) Painting the model comes last.

2. (T/F) The guide says instructions are not important.

3. (T/F) A large, empty table would be a good workspace.

4. (T/F) To build the model, special glue is used.

Dictation

A. Listen and fill in the blanks. Track 13

Maya: What are you 1( )?

Kenji: I'm making a birdhouse. Some bluebirds and robins live nearby.

Maya: Are you going to 2( ) them?

Kenji: Yes, exactly. They can also go inside the house. It gets 3( ) around here.

Maya: That's very nice of you. It looks great so far.

Kenji: Thanks! I'm learning from a YouTube video. It teaches you everything 4( ).

B. Choose the best answer.

1. ( ) Kenji says the area ______.
   A: is sometimes cold
   B: has more bluebirds than robins
   C: needs several more birdhouses
   D: isn't usually windy

2. ( ) Why is Kenji making a birdhouse?
   A: To make a YouTube video
   B: To give it to Maya
   C: To teach friends about robins
   D: To feed nearby birds

Discussion

Discuss these questions together.

1. Do you like making things by hand? If so, what do you make?
2. What kinds of handmade items do people sell?
3. Do you own any handmade items? If so, what are they?

7 Cooking

Part 1: I love to cook.

Read the following story. Track 14

My name is Amy. I love to cook. I make soups, rice dishes, and much more. I also enjoy learning to cook new dishes. Desserts are my favorite things to make. People love my cookies. They're big, but not too sweet.

I often cook for other people. Sometimes, my best friend comes over. I make dinner for her. On weekends, I cook lunch for my brother. He's like me. He loves desserts!

Vocabulary Check

Write the correct word in each blank.

weekend	dessert	cook	favorite

1. We visit our grandfather every ___________.
2. It takes 40 minutes to ___________ the dish.
3. Can we have strawberry ice cream for ___________?
4. What's your ___________ kind of fruit?

Reading Check

Choose the best answer.

1. (   ) When does Amy's best friend go to her house?
   A: Before lunchtime
   B: At night
   C: On Saturday and Sunday
   D: Every day

2. (   ) Amy loves cooking ____________.
   A: many kinds of food   B: rice dishes, but not soups
   C: very few things   D: sweet things only

3. (   ) "They're big, but not too sweet." What are "they"?
   A: Amy's rice dishes
   B: Amy's dinners
   C: Amy's soups
   D: Amy's cookies

4. (   ) Why does Amy's brother like her cooking?
   A: She makes good desserts.
   B: She cooks for him every day.
   C: She gets along with him.
   D: She makes very sweet things.

Grammar Check

Write the correct word in each blank.

Ex: This is our favorite park. We come here ___*often*___**.**
(never / often)

1. I dislike carrots. I ______________ eat them.
   (often/never)

2. We __________________ cook together. We do that almost every day.
   (sometimes/often)

3. My boss ____________________ drinks coffee – about once a week.
   (never/sometimes)

4. Billy ________________ walks the dog. It's his job.
   (always/never)

Part 2: Making Chocolate Chip Cookies

Look at the following recipe.

Recipe #23 Chocolate Chip Cookies

Ingredients:

2 cups of chocolate chips
1 teaspoon of baking soda
1 teaspoon of vanilla
2 1/2 cups of flour
3/4 cup of white sugar
1 cup of brown sugar
2 eggs
1 teaspoon of salt
1 cup of butter

Directions:

1) Preheat the oven to 190 degrees C.
2) Use a large bowl to mix the butter, white sugar, and brown sugar.
3) Mix in the eggs, one at a time. Stir in the vanilla.
4) In a small bowl, mix the salt, baking soda, and flour. Then, pour it all into the large bowl.
5) Add the chocolate chips to the large bowl.
6) Put spoonfulls of the finished mix onto a baking pan.
7) Bake for 10 minutes.

True or False

Circle true (T) or false (F).

1. (T/F) There are seven steps in the directions.
2. (T/F) Less than one cup of white sugar is needed.
3. (T/F) You mix the salt, baking soda, and flour in a large bowl.
4. (T/F) The chocolate chips are added before the eggs.

Dictation

A. Listen and fill in the blanks. Track 15

Michael: What should we cook for $_1$(   )?

Emily: How about a pasta dish? My grandmother's $_2$(   ) is full of recipes.

Michael: OK. I can make a soup or salad to go with it.

Emily: Hmm...It's a little cold. Soup would $_3$(   ).

Michael: Soup it is, then. I'll use $_4$(   ) and green peppers from the garden.

Emily: Sounds delicious!

B. Choose the best answer.

1. (   ) The pasta recipes are from ________.
   A: Michael
   B: Michael's mother
   C: Emily
   D: Emily's grandmother

2. (   ) Why does Emily want soup?
   A: She is really hungry.
   B: The house is cold.
   C: Michael has a new recipe.
   D: They always eat salad.

Discussion

Discuss these questions together.

1. What are your favorite things to eat?
2. Do you usually eat at home or at restaurants?
3. Do you like to cook?

8 Sports

Part 1: Basketball

Read the following article. Track 16

Basketball is played by boys, girls, men, and women all over the world. To play, you only need a basketball and a court.

The basic rules of the game are simple. Just shoot the ball into the basket. Also, you can't run with the ball. You must bounce it on the court.

For basketball players, it helps to be tall. But it isn't necessary. Many great players are average height or smaller.

Vocabulary Check

Write the correct word in each blank.

world	rule	simple	run

1. You ____________ so fast. The track team is lucky to have you.
2. There are more than 100 countries in the ____________.
3. The library has one important ____________: Don't talk loudly.
4. It's a ____________ meal. We can make it in a few minutes.

Reading Check

Choose the best answer.

1. (   ) Who likes to play basketball?
   A: Only young people
   B: Mostly older people
   C: People of all ages
   D: Men and boys only

2. (   ) Basketball players cannot __________ the ball.
   A: run and carry
   B: bounce
   C: shoot
   D: hold

3. (   ) What is "it" in the second paragraph?
   A: the ball
   B: the court
   C: the game
   D: the basket

4. (   ) Which of these is true?
   A: The basic rules of basketball are hard to learn.
   B: Every great basketball player is tall.
   C: To play the game, you only need a basketball.
   D: Players bounce the ball during a game.

Grammar Check

Put the words in the correct order.

1. (exciting / Basketball / sport / an / is)

   ____.

2. (watch / the game / my house / We / at / can)

   ____.

3. (another / plays / on / Lisa / team)

   ____.

Part 2: Opinions about Sports

Read the following statements.

What do you think about sports?

Jessica: I love sports. I play soccer with my friends on Fridays.

Minh: I don't play any sports. But I like to watch them on TV.

Carlos: I mostly play sports to have fun. Winning is nice. If I lose, that's also fine.

Abdul: Actually, I'm not interested in sports. I don't like them or hate them.

True or False

Circle true (T) or false (F).

1. (T/F) Two of these people play sports.
2. (T/F) On the weekend, Minh might watch a game with Abdul.
3. (T/F) For Carlos, winning is the most important thing.
4. (T/F) Jessica plays soccer every week.

Dictation

A. Listen and fill in the blanks. Track 17

Carol: Do you want to play tennis? I just got a new racket.

Bill: Sure. Do you have an 1(   ) racket?

Carol: Just my old one. But it's in 2(   ).

Bill: That works for me. I can play for about an hour. Then I'm 3(   ) my mom for lunch.

Carol: Great. Your mom is good at tennis, isn't she?

Bill: Much better than me. You should 4(   ) sometime.

B. Choose the best answer.

1. (   ) Bill wants to ________.
   A: meet his friend's mom
   B: buy some tennis balls
   C: have lunch with Carol
   D: use one of Carol's rackets

2. (   ) What does Bill suggest?
   A: Carol and his mom should play tennis.
   B: He and Carol should play for two hours.
   C: The two friends should make dinner plans.
   D: First, they should shop for new rackets.

Discussion

Discuss these questions together.

1. Do you play any sports? If so, which ones?

2. Which sports, if any, do you like to watch?

3. How can someone become good at a sport?

9 Natural Places and Maps

Part 1: The Amazon River

Read the following article. Track 18

The Amazon River is special for a lot of reasons. It's 6,400 kilometers long. That makes it the world's second longest river. It's also the home of many plants, animals, and fish. Plus, it goes through the world's largest rainforest.

The Amazon also moves through seven countries in South America. It's a big river with plenty of secrets. We're still learning about them.

Vocabulary Check

Write the correct word(s) in each blank.

plenty of	country	river	secret

1. Do you want to go swimming in the ____________?

2. India is a big ____________. It has more than one billion people.

3. We have ____________ time. There's no hurry.

4. Sorry, I can't tell you. It's a ____________.

Reading Check

Choose the best answer.

1. (   ) How many countries does the Amazon go through?
   A: 2
   B: 7
   C: 4,000
   D: 6,400

2. (   ) The article does not say the Amazon is full of ________.
   A: people
   B: fish
   C: animals
   D: plants

3. (   ) What does the article suggest?
   A: We know everything about South America.
   B: The Amazon doesn't have any more secrets.
   C: The Amazon is the world's longest river.
   D: It takes time to learn all about the Amazon.

4. (   ) Which of these is true?
   A: The Amazon is 16,400 kilometers long.
   B: The Amazon goes through a very big rainforest.
   C: The Amazon is like many rivers around the world.
   D: The Amazon is in North America.

Grammar Check

Put the words in the correct order.

1. (boats / learning / I / about / am)

   ________________________________.

2. (in / There / many / fish / the river / are)

   ________________________________.

3. (tallest / is / This / world's / the / tree)

   ________________________________.

Part 2: Map of Jefferson County

Look at the following map.

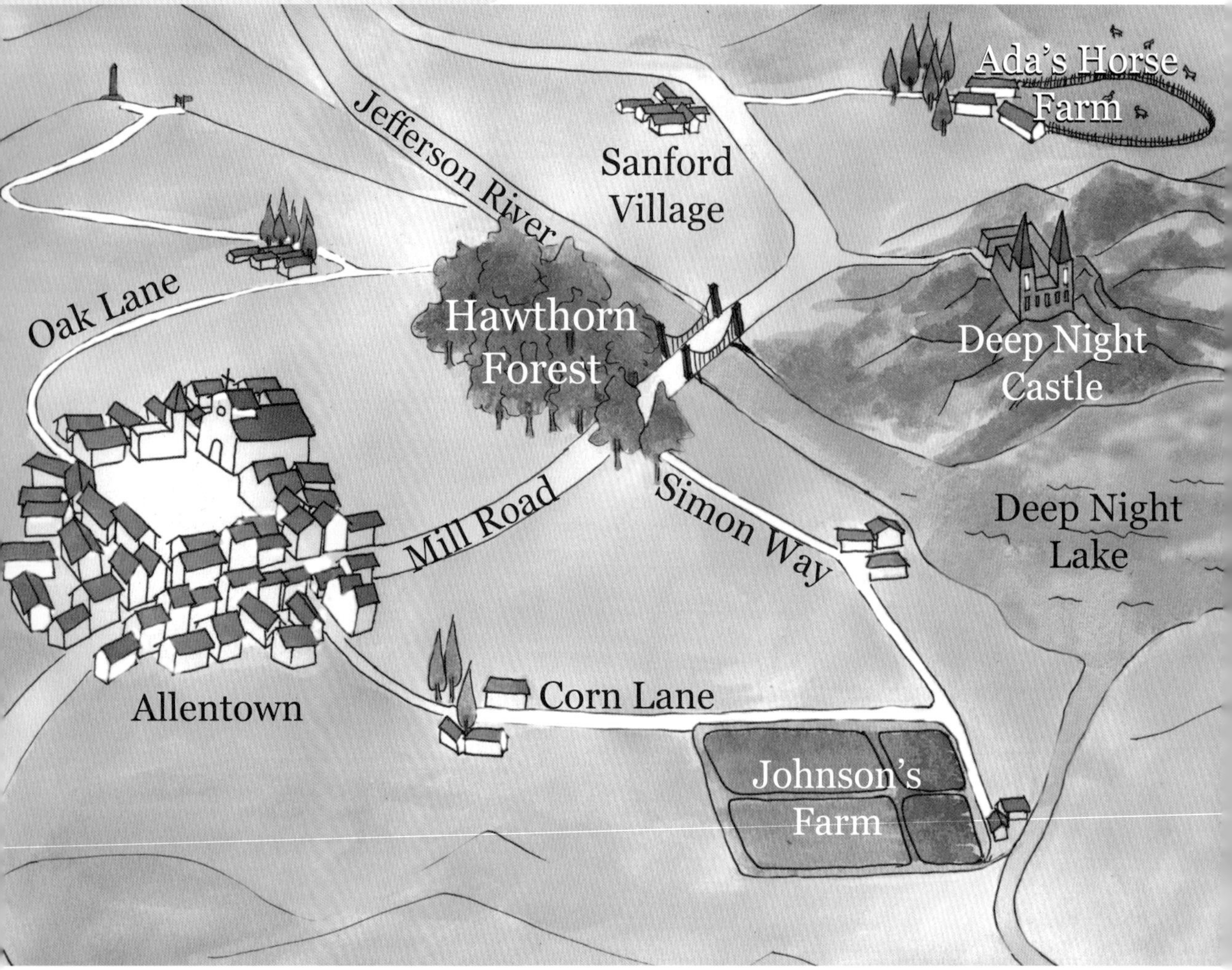

True or False

Circle true (T) or false (F).

1. (T/F) Hawthorn Forest is along Jefferson River.

2. (T/F) Johnson's Farm is next to Ada's Horse Farm.

3. (T/F) Corn Lane goes from Allentown to Sanford Village.

4. (T/F) The castle and the lake have the same name.

Dictation

A. Listen and fill in the blanks. Track 19

Martin: 1( ). Is there a post office near here?

Kayo: Yes, there is. Do you see the convenience store 2( )?

Martin: I do, yes.

Kayo: Make a right at the store. Then, 3( )...let me see...about 50 meters. You'll see the post office on your left.

Martin: That's easy enough. Thank you 4( ).

Kayo: My pleasure. Have a great day.

Martin: You, too!

B. Choose the best answer.

1. ( ) Martin probably wants to ______.
   A: get some coffee
   B: send a letter
   C: buy a map
   D: go shopping

2. ( ) What does Kayo tell Martin to do?
   A: Take a train to the post office
   B: Walk 0.5 kilometers
   C: Ask another person for help
   D: Turn right at a store

Discussion

Discuss these questions together.

1. In your area, are there any nice rivers or lakes?
2. Do people ever ask you for directions? Are you good at giving directions?
3. Do you ever get lost? What do you do in those situations?

10 Dreams and Seasons

Part 1: Space Dreams

Read the following story. Track 20

Linus has big dreams. He doesn't want a normal job in a tall building. Linus wants to work much higher up – in space. He thinks about it all the time. He also follows the news about space.

Linus could work on a space station. Or, he might fly a spaceship. He could even travel to Mars. Day and night, Linus dreams with stars in his eyes.

Vocabulary Check

Write the correct word in each blank.

building	space	normal	fly

1. We plan to ____________ from Bangkok to Singapore.

2. My office is in that ____________ over there.

3. This is ____________ weather for May.

4. Do you ever look up at the stars in ____________?

Reading Check

Choose the best answer.

1. (   ) When does Linus think about space?
   A: Day and night
   B: Only when reading the news
   C: Usually just before sleeping
   D: Mostly at school

2. (   ) Which space-related job is not in the story?
   A: Flying a spaceship
   B: Traveling to another planet
   C: Building homes on the moon
   D: Working on a space station

3. (   ) What do we know about Linus?
   A: He is learning about space in school.
   B: He is already training to live in space.
   C: He knows about the latest space news.
   D: He likes studying stars more than planets.

4. (   ) What would Linus say about a job at a bank?
   A: "It's better than working in space."
   B: "That's my dream job!"
   C: "I can make a lot of money there."
   D: "It's not for me."

Grammar Check

Complete each sentence with *could*, *want*, or *can't*.

Ex: It's snowing. We ___*can't*___ play baseball today.

1. I ________ to go with you. But I have to finish my homework.

2. Excuse me, Peter. ________ I speak with you?

3. Sorry, we ________ go out. We have to stay home.

4. Yes, she ________ become a nurse. But she wants to be a pilot.

Part 2: Different Seasons

Read the following story.

In the spring, I spend a lot of time outside. I like smelling the new flowers.

In the summer, I often go to the beach. I also eat a lot of ice cream.

In the fall, I like picking apples. Fresh apples taste great!

In the winter, I usually stay inside. Sometimes, I go shopping.

True or False

Circle true (T) or false (F).

1. (T/F) She likes cold desserts in the summer.
2. (T/F) She loves the smell of flowers in the spring.
3. (T/F) In January, she probably goes shopping every day.
4. (T/F) Apple picking in the winter is a lot of fun.

Dictation

A. Listen and fill in the blanks. Track 21

Rico: Look at these flower buds. Spring is 1(   )!

Dana: I can't wait. We need some 2(   ) days and sunshine.

Rico: Winter is too long, for sure. Still, I kind of like the snow.

Dana: It is pretty. My little brother loves 3(   ) snowmen.

Rico: That's so much fun. Anyway, what should we do in the warmer weather?

Dana: First things first. Let's go to the 4(   )!

B. Choose the best answer.

1. (   ) Dana's brother and Rico ________.
   A: enjoy making snowmen
   B: love going to the beach
   C: sometimes give Dana flowers
   D: don't like the winter

2. (   ) Why does Rico think spring is coming?
   A: It isn't snowing anymore.
   B: The sky is clear.
   C: He sees some flower buds.
   D: It's getting hot.

Discussion

Discuss these questions together.

1. Are you interested in any space news? (Ex: the International Space Station, missions to Mars, etc.)
2. Do you have any big dreams or goals? If so, what are they?
3. What is your favorite season? Why?

11 Culture

Part 1: The Culture of Canada: The Stampede

Read the following article. Track 22

The Calgary Stampede is a major event in Canada. Every July, more than one million people attend.

At the Stampede, there is a big rodeo. Riders show their horse and bull riding skills.

There are also farm animal shows, art shows, and more. What an event! Canadians call it "The Greatest Outdoor Show on Earth."

Vocabulary Check

Write the correct word in each blank.

attend	farm	skill	show

1. The Hendersons grow corn and potatoes on their ____________.
2. This Sunday, I will ____________ a friend's wedding.
3. Are you going to the big car ____________ next month?
4. Flying an airplane takes a lot of ____________.

Reading Check

Choose the best answer.

1. (   ) About how many people attend the Stampede yearly?
   A: 1,000
   B: 100,000
   C: 1,000,000
   D: 10,000,000

2. (   ) What happens at a rodeo?
   A: People sell animals.
   B: People ride horses and bulls.
   C: People make art.
   D: People visit Canada.

3. (   ) The article does not have information about ________.
   A: the month of the Stampede
   B: the Stampede's country
   C: the Stampede's events
   D: the cost to attend the Stampede

4. (   ) Which of these does the Stampede have?
   A: Rodeos with one million horses
   B: Shows with animals in them
   C: Free bull riding classes
   D: Horse and other animal races

Grammar Check

Write the correct form of each word.

Ex: Kids love *attending* (attend) the event.

1. ________ (Dance) at the club was so exciting.

2. The bracelet is pretty. You're a great jewelry ________ (make).

3. I would never ride a bull. It's too ________ (danger).

4. Mary wants to be a ________ (farm). She has a green thumb.

Part 2: Meeting a Foreign Exchange Student

Read the following conversation.

True or False

Circle true (T) or false (F).

1. (T/ F) It's their first time meeting.

2. (T/ F) Hanna and Luis are in the same class.

3. (T/ F) Luis spoke English growing up.

4. (T/ F) Luis asks Hanna for help.

Dictation

A. Listen and fill in the blanks. Track 23

Jerry: There's a new study abroad program. Imagine living in 1(   ) for six weeks.

Imelda: Sounds like a dream summer. Which 2(   ) is it in?

Jerry: You can go to Sweden, Holland, or France.

Imelda: Is it all studying?

Jerry: There are 3(   ) and culture classes for five weeks. Then you take a one-week tour.

Imelda: I'd love to get 4(   ). Hopefully it isn't too expensive.

B. Choose the best answer.

1. (   ) Students take classes in Europe for ________ week(s).
   A: one B: two
   C: five D: six

2. (   ) Which of these is true?
   A: Jerry plans to go to Holland or France.
   B: Students all study in the same country.
   C: The program teaches you about the culture.
   D: Imelda is not worried about the price.

Discussion

Discuss these questions together.

1. Have you ever been to a big event like the Stampede?
2. Do you know any students from other countries? Which places?
3. What's good about studying in another country? Are there any bad points?

12 Music

Part 1: Yo-Yo Ma

Read the following article. Track 24

Yo-Yo Ma is a top cellist. He gives concerts around the world. Sometimes, he plays on TV shows like the Academy Awards. He also records a lot of music.

Yo-Yo Ma loves learning new musical styles. He plays classical music, folk music, tangos, and more. His playing is full of feeling. Yo-Yo Ma's concerts and albums are very popular. And he is friendly to his fans.

Vocabulary Check

Write the correct word in each blank.

around	concert	feeling	friendly

1. My uncle is ____________. Everybody likes him.
2. What's your ____________ about this statue? Do you like it?
3. I love walking ____________ here. It's so quiet.
4. The jazz ____________ was incredible. We danced the whole time.

Reading Check

Choose the best answer.

1. ( ) Yo-Yo Ma plays the cello __________.
   A: in many countries
   B: in the USA only
   C: on other worlds
   D: in just a few places

2. ( ) What do we learn about Yo-Yo Ma's fans?
   A: Yo-Yo Ma gives them concert tickets.
   B: Yo-Yo Ma is kind to them.
   C: Yo-Yo Ma worries about them.
   D: Yo-Yo Ma records music with them.

3. ( ) Why does the article mention the Academy Awards?
   A: To show how Yo-Yo Ma wins a lot of awards
   B: To suggest a good store with the best music
   C: To tell readers about a music recording studio
   D: To give an example of a TV show with Yo-Yo Ma

4. ( ) The article does not say Yo-Yo Ma plays __________.
   A: folk music
   B: tangos
   C: pop music
   D: classical music

Grammar Check

Complete each sentence with *he*, *his*, or *him*.

Ex: ___*He*___ is a great soccer player.

1. Is this __________ bag?

2. Jack is my best friend. __________ lives near me.

3. Mr. Simons looks busy. We can ask __________ the question later.

4. That's __________ violin. It's 100 years old.

Part 2: Music Sales

Read the following information.

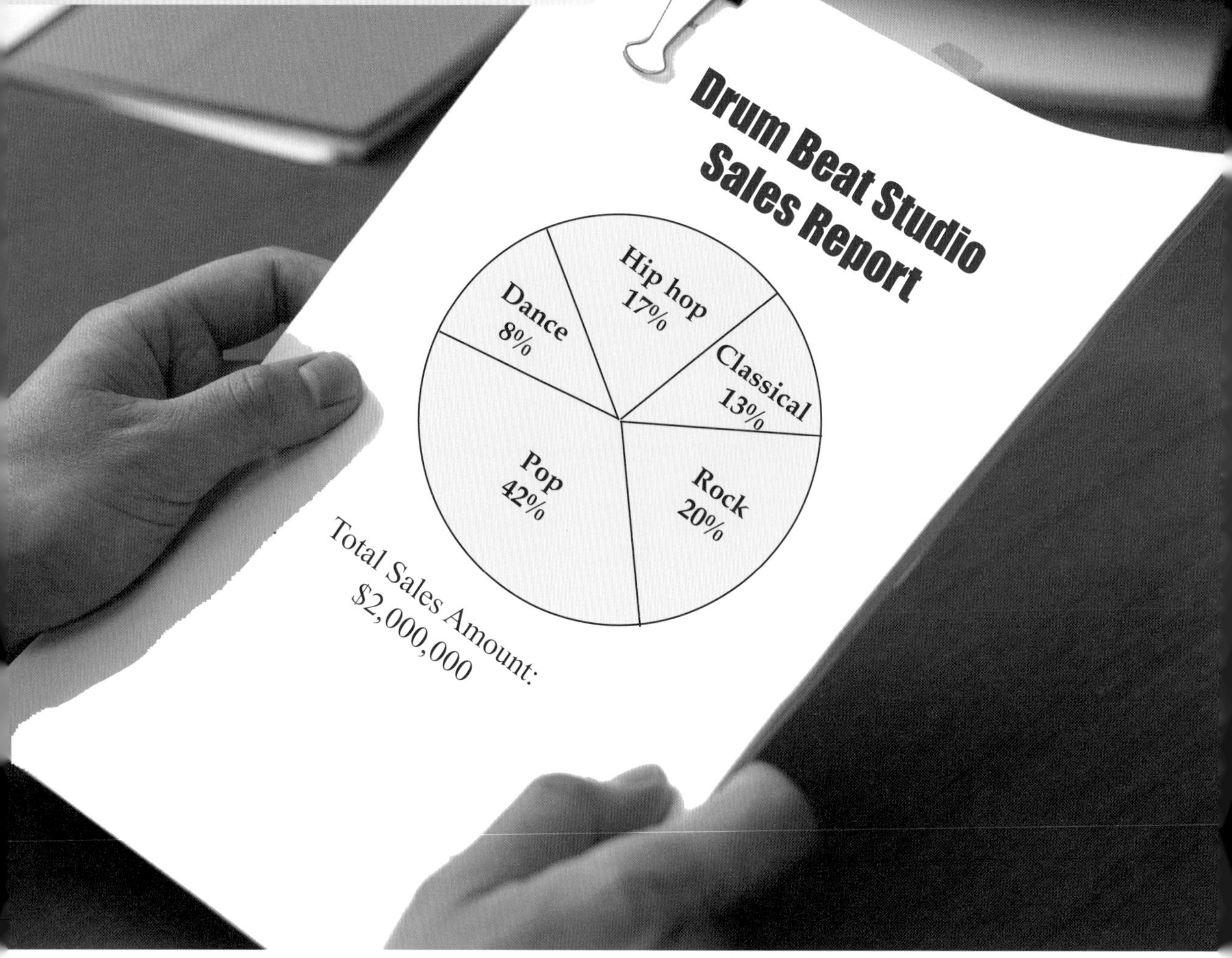

True or False

Circle true (T) or false (F).

1. (T/F) The studio makes five kinds of music.
2. (T/F) Most of their sales are from dance music.
3. (T/F) Rock music sells better than hip hop.
4. (T/F) Classical music makes up 31% of the sales.

Dictation

A. Listen and fill in the blanks. Track 25

Tom: Finally, I get to see my favorite 1(   ) live.

Erin: It's so exciting! I still have their poster on my wall.

Tom: The show starts in 2(   ). Do you want to get anything first?

Erin: Just a drink. How about you?

Tom: A concert T-shirt and 3(   ) a hat. A soda would be good, too.

Erin: OK. Go find the concert stuff. 4(   ) get the drinks.

B. Choose the best answer.

1. (   ) Tom does not want a ________.
   A: hat
   B: drink
   C: poster
   D: shirt

2. (   ) What do we learn about Erin?
   A: She often sees the band live.
   B: She is going to buy Tom a soda.
   C: She may be 20 minutes late.
   D: She is wearing a concert T-shirt.

Discussion

Discuss these questions together.

1. What is your favorite kind of music?
2. Do you play any instruments? (Ex: piano, violin, guitar)
3. Do you often watch live concerts?

13 Mountains

Part 1: Mount Fuji

Read the following article. Track 26

Mount Fuji, in central Japan, is a resting volcano. It hasn't erupted in more than 300 years. In winter, the top is covered with snow. Often, the area is cloudy. Then, Fuji-san hides in the clouds.

Mount Fuji is an important symbol of Japan. It is also like an old friend to the Japanese. Fuji-san is in many poems and stories. Also, there are many paintings of the mountain.

Vocabulary Check

Write the correct word in each blank.

hide	snow	painting	cloudy

1. I don't like walking in the ____________. It's cold and wet.

2. It's so ____________ today. The sky is totally white.

3. This ____________ is my favorite. I love the dark colors.

4. My cat likes to ____________ in here. Sometimes, I can't find her!

Reading Check

Choose the best answer.

1. (   ) When is it hard to see Mount Fuji?
   A: During cold months
   B: Only when it's sunny
   C: When snow covers the top
   D: In cloudy weather

2. (   ) The article does not say Mount Fuji is in many ___________.
   A: stories
   B: paintings
   C: poems
   D: video games

3. (   ) In the second paragraph, what does "It" mean?
   A: Japan B: Your best friend
   C: Mount Fuji D: A different volcano

4. (   ) What does the article say about Japan?
   A: The people are scared of Mount Fuji.
   B: The people rarely visit Mount Fuji.
   C: The people write about Mount Fuji.
   D: The people don't care about Mount Fuji.

Grammar Check

Write the correct word in each blank.

Ex: These flowers ___*are*___ so pretty.
(is / are)

1. The park ___________ full of rose bushes.
   (is/are)

2. That cloud looks ___________ a fish!
   (like/likes)

3. It's a lovely day. We don't need to ___________ inside.
   (stay/stays)

4. The tables ___________ covered with books.
   (is/are)

Read the following information.

There are many famous mountains in the world. They are important to local cultures. And visitors from everywhere love seeing them. Climbing famous mountains is also popular. However, for some giant mountains, it is hard to reach the top.

Here is some information about five famous mountains.

Name	Height	Interesting Fact
Mount Everest	8,848 m	World's tallest mountain
Mount Kilimanjaro	5,895 m	Home to elephants and giraffes
Mont Blanc	4,808 m	First climbed in 1786
Mount Fuji	3,776 m	More than 200,000 yearly climbers
Mount Olympus	2,919 m	In Greek stories, 12 gods live there.

True or False

Circle true (T) or false (F).

1. (T/F) Famous mountains are only popular with local visitors.
2. (T/F) The height of Mount Fuji is 3,776 meters.
3. (T/F) Climbers can see giraffes on Mount Everest.
4. (T/F) Exactly 12 people went up Mount Olympus in 1786.

Dictation

A. Listen and fill in the blanks. Track 27

Marta: I love hiking in these mountains.

Tim: The scenery is beautiful. We should come here 1( ).

Marta: I agree. It's just an hour's drive from the city. Hey, 2( ) the nest up there.

Tim: Oh yeah, I see it now. This could be a nice spot for lunch.

Marta: I am so hungry after all that walking. Here's 3( ) for any garbage.

Tim: 4( ). We don't want to leave anything behind.

B. Choose the best answer.

1. ( ) They plan to take ________ home.
   A: the nest B: some leaves
   C: any garbage D: their lunch

2. ( ) Which of these is true?
   A: They want to visit the mountains more.
   B: It takes them half a day to drive there.
   C: Marta doesn't live in the city anymore.
   D: They are going to eat lunch in their car.

Discussion

Discuss these questions together.

1. Do you enjoy going to parks?
2. Do you ever go hiking? If so, where do you like to go?
3. Are you interested in visiting any famous mountains? If so, which ones?

14 Weekends

Part 1: Ways to Spend the Weekend

Read the following story. Track 28

Tina has two days off each week: Saturday and Sunday. One morning, she likes to read the news online. The other morning, she goes jogging.

On weekend afternoons, Tina sees friends or talks on the phone.

At night, Tina likes going to nice restaurants and seeing shows. But those things are expensive. She can only choose one of them each week.

Vocabulary Check

Write the correct word in each blank.

jog	expensive	choose	morning

1. We have breakfast together every ______________.
2. The art pieces are ______________. I'll put them somewhere safe.
3. It's a nice place to ______________. It's pretty, and there are no cars.
4. I need to ______________ a jacket. Which one goes with these pants?

Reading Check

Choose the best answer.

1. (　　) On Saturday at 3:30 PM, Tina might ________.
   A: talk to her best friend　　B: exercise
   C: read something　　D: see a show

2. (　　) During one weekend, Tina cannot ________.
   A: go jogging and talk on the phone
   B: go to a restaurant and see a show
   C: talk to friends and eat at a restaurant
   D: talk on the phone and see a show

3. (　　) Today is Saturday. Tina is reading the news. What might Tina do the next morning?
   A: Read the news again
   B: Go running
   C: Wake up late
   D: See a friend

4. (　　) Which of these might Tina do on a Sunday evening?
   A: Read the news
   B: Talk on the phone
   C: Go to a restaurant
   D: Visit somebody

Grammar Check

Write the correct word(s) in each blank.

Ex: Usually, I exercise in ___*the morning*___.
(morning / the morning)

1. I like to relax on ________________.
   (weekend / the weekend)

2. It gets a little cold here at ________________.
   (night / the night)

3. During ________________, we work hard.
   (day / the day)

4. My aunt sleeps for an hour in ________________.
   (afternoon / the afternoon)

Part 2: Buying Movie Tickets

Read the following conversation.

Cashier:	How can I help you?
Customer:	Two tickets for *The Big Find*, please.
Cashier:	For the 3:30 show?
Customer:	Yes, that's right.
Cashier:	We have a ticket deal. For $25, you can get two movie tickets, two drinks, and two bags of popcorn.
Customer:	Sure, that's a good deal. Here's $50.
Cashier:	Thank you. $25 is your change.

True or False

Circle true (T) or false (F).

1. (T/F) The customer buys the tickets at 3:00 PM. The movie will start in 30 minutes.

2. (T/F) The cashier offers a special deal.

3. (T/F) The customer will receive six things to eat.

4. (T/F) The cashier hands the customer $50.

Dictation

A. Listen and fill in the blanks. Track 29

Mei-lin: What should we do today?

Brett: I want to 1(   ). But I don't have any money.

Mei-lin: I 2(   ). We could go to the beach.

Brett: I like the sound of that! There isn't a cloud in the sky. I can 3(   ).

Mei-lin: And I can 4(   ) some iced tea. I also have a big towel to sit on.

Brett: Perfect.

B. Choose the best answer.

1. (   ) The friends do not have something to ________.
   A: drink
   B: sit on
   C: eat
   D: read

2. (   ) What does Brett say about the weather?
   A: It might rain.
   B: It's a little cloudy.
   C: The sky is clear.
   D: It's very hot.

Discussion

Discuss these questions together.

1. What do you usually do on the weekend?

2. What are some free things to do for fun?

3. Do you like going to the beach?

15 Transportation

Part 1: This Old Car

Read the following story. Track 30

My car is more than 30 years old. I use it all the time. In fact, I probably drive it two hours a day. The car isn't fast. And it's not very nice to look at.

But you know, I really love this car. It runs well. And I take good care of it. I treat it like an old friend. This old car and I have a long history together.

Vocabulary Check

Write the correct word in each blank.

together	probably	drive	treat

1. I ____________ my friends well. They are important to me.

2. It will ____________ rain later. I'll take my umbrella.

3. Laura and her cousin go everywhere ____________.

4. Do you want to ____________ downtown? Or should we take a train?

Reading Check

Choose the best answer.

1. (   ) What is the car like?
   A: Fast but ugly
   B: Nice looking but old
   C: New but slow
   D: Old but good

2. (   ) How does the man feel about his car?
   A: He wants a new one.
   B: He wants to keep it.
   C: He wants to fix it.
   D: He wants to give it away.

3. (   ) Why does the car still run well?
   A: The man treats it well.
   B: It's better than most new cars.
   C: It likes the man.
   D: The man drives it fast.

4. (   ) Which of these is like the man and his car?
   A: A woman living in an old house
   B: Two people at a company
   C: A doctor and a nurse working together
   D: A man and a new airplane

Grammar Check

Write the correct form of each word.
Use the present tense.

Ex: Danny ___*takes*___ (take) the bus to school every day.

1. Her sister __________ (be) 17 years old.

2. Joan __________ (treat) everybody kindly.

3. You __________ (take) great care of your things.

4. Mr. Ueda and his son __________ (love) fixing old cars.

Part 2: Poll - Ways to Get Around

Read the following poll.

We want to understand how people get around. Please check one answer to each question.

1. What's your favorite kind of private transportation?
   - ☐ Bicycle
   - ☐ Car
   - ☐ Motorcycle
2. What's your favorite kind of public transportation?
   - ☐ Train
   - ☐ Bus
   - ☐ Subway
3. How often do you use the subway?
   - ☐ Once a week (or less)
   - ☐ 2-4 times a week
   - ☐ 5-6 times a week (or more)
4. How much do you walk every day?
   - ☐ 10-30 minutes
   - ☐ 30 minutes to one hour
   - ☐ More than an hour

Current Results

1.	Bicycle	43%		
	Car	38%		
	Motorcycle	19%		
2.	Train	31%		
	Bus	26%		
	Subway	43%		
3.	Once a week (or less)	12%		
	2-4 times a week	31%		
	5-6 times a week (or more)	57%		
4.	10-30 minutes	18%		
	30 minutes to one hour	62%		
	More than an hour	20%		

True or False

Circle true (T) or false (F).

1. (T/F) The poll asks about public and private transportation.
2. (T/F) There is a question about safety.
3. (T/F) More than 25% of people prefer the bus.
4. (T/F) Most people walk 30 to 60 minutes a day.

Dictation

A. Listen and fill in the blanks. Track 31

Tim: The 1( ) game starts in exactly two hours. Do you want to take a bus there?

Leila: Hmm...It's 5:20 now. Traffic might be 2( ).

Tim: Good point. We could 3( ) to Oakfield Station. From there, it's a 15-minute walk to the stadium.

Leila: That works. It's a 4( ) for a walk.

Tim: It sure is. Plus, I need the exercise.

Leila: Me, too!

B. Choose the best answer.

1. ( ) Leila is worried about ________.
   A: being in traffic
   B: walking too far
   C: getting lost
   D: taking a train

2. ( ) They want to be at the stadium on time. What time do they need to arrive at Oakfield Station?
   A: 5:20 B: 7:05
   C: 7:20 D: 9:00

Discussion

Discuss these questions together.

1. How do you usually get around? (Ex: bike, bus, train)
2. What's good about taking public transportation? Are there any bad points?
3. Do you want to own a car someday? Why or why not?

16 Dragons and Folktales

Part 1: Dragons: East Vs. West

Read the following article. Track 32

There are many stories about dragons. Countries have different feelings about these creatures. In stories from the East and West, dragons are not at all the same.

In Western stories, dragons are usually bad. They steal gold. They also breathe fire and hurt people.

In Eastern stories, dragons are smart and friendly. They help people. Finding a dragon is very good luck.

Vocabulary Check

Write the correct word in each blank.

same	find	gold	hurt

1. That looks just like my bag. It's the ______________ style and color.

2. Joe can't ______________ his watch. Do you know where it is?

3. I ______________ my back playing rugby. I need to rest today.

4. What a lovely ring. Is it made of ______________?

Reading Check

Choose the best answer.

1. (   ) In Western stories, what do dragons take from people?
   A: Feelings
   B: Countries
   C: Fire
   D: Gold

2. (   ) Dragons in Eastern stories are not __________.
   A: bad
   B: friendly
   C: lucky
   D: smart

3. (   ) Which of these is probably true?
   A: In Eastern stories, people don't want to meet dragons.
   B: Drawings of Western and Eastern dragons are the same.
   C: People in Western stories are afraid of dragons.
   D: Only one or two countries have dragon stories.

4. (   ) "...dragons are not at all the same." What does "not at all" mean?
   A: at times
   B: mostly
   C: totally not
   D: always

Grammar Check

Write the correct form of each word.

Ex: The house is behind a store. ___*Finding*___ (Find) it is a little hard.

1. Our neighbor is such a __________ (friend) person.

2. What's your __________ (feel) about the design?

3. I __________ (usual) wake up at 7:00.

4. You have the winning number. You're so __________ (luck)!

Look at the following table of contents.

Contents

All about Dragons

True or False

Circle true (T) or false (F).

1. (T/F) The book is only about dragons from long ago.
2. (T/F) You can probably see drawings in Part 3.
3. (T/F) On page 88, you might learn about a good movie.
4. (T/F) The chapter about fire is less than 10 pages long.

Dictation

A. Listen and fill in the blanks. Track 33

Caroline: I'm 1(   ) an old Chinese folktale. It's called "Mulan."

Bob: That's a 2(   ) story, isn't it?

Caroline: It is, and Mulan is a 3(   ). I like that a lot.

Bob: Let me think.... There's a movie about the story, right?

Caroline: Yes, and some cartoons, too. I'm 4(   ) with the book. Do you want to borrow it tomorrow?

Bob: I'd love to, thanks.

B. Choose the best answer.

1. (   ) What does Caroline say about Mulan?
   A: There is a Mulan cartoon, but no movies.
   B: The story is from China.
   C: Caroline's friends all know the folktale.
   D: It's a brand new story.

2. (   ) Tomorrow, Bob is going to ____________.
   A: watch a cartoon
   B: borrow a book
   C: travel to China
   D: see a movie

Discussion

Discuss these questions together.

1. What kinds of books do you like?

2. Do you enjoy stories about dragons or other creatures?

3. Do you have any favorite folktales? If so, what are they?

17 Typhoons

Part 1: Typhoon Basics

Read the following article. Track 34

A typhoon is a strong weather system. It starts above the ocean. Its winds go around and around. Slowly, the typhoon moves across the ocean.

Often, typhoons pass over land. They bring strong winds – up to 200 kilometers per hour. They also bring heavy rains. For big storms, the rainfall may total 500 mm or more. In this dangerous weather, people must be very careful.

Vocabulary Check

Write the correct word in each blank.

dangerous	strong	weather	starts

1. The party ______________ at 7:30.
2. The children shouldn't play in the street. It's ______________.
3. I love sunny ______________. It makes me feel great.
4. You look ______________. Can you open this window?

Reading Check

Choose the best answer.

1. ( ) Where does a typhoon start?
   A: Somewhere above the ocean
   B: On the beach
   C: In a different weather system
   D: Near land

2. ( ) A typhoon is a ________ weather system.
   A: cold
   B: dangerous
   C: dry
   D: safe

3. ( ) What happens last?
   A: A typhoon goes around and around.
   B: A typhoon brings strong winds to a country.
   C: A typhoon starts away from the land.
   D: A typhoon moves across the ocean.

4. ( ) Which of these is true?
   A: Typhoons often bring 200 meters of rain.
   B: Typhoon winds move like a circle.
   C: Typhoons always pass over land.
   D: Typhoons move 1,000 kilometers per hour.

Grammar Check

Put the words in the correct order.

1. (large / It's / storm / very / a)

   ____.

2. (the / walking / They / street / are / across)

   ____.

3. (becoming / winds / The / stronger / are)

   ____.

Part 2: Preparing for a Typhoon

Read the following information.

Being ready for a typhoon is important.
Here are some good tips to follow.

1. Follow the weather reports closely.

2. **Before the typhoon:**
   - Buy food, water, and supplies.
   - Charge your phone and other items.
   - Make sure all your windows are closed.

3. Stay inside during the typhoon.

4. After the typhoon, be careful. (There may be tree branches and glass on the street.)

True or False

Circle true (T) or false (F).

1. (T/F) Charge the flashlight batteries before the typhoon.

2. (T/F) Always keep one window open for fresh air.

3. (T/F) Buying supplies during a typhoon is fine.

4. (T/F) There are dangers to avoid after a typhoon.

Dictation

A. Listen and fill in the blanks. Track 35

Lydia: Wow, the rain is really coming down. Listen to that 1( ).

Victor: It sure is strong. You know, I'm still kind of 2( ).

Lydia: Don't we have some snacks?

Victor: They're all gone. I could run to the convenience store.

Lydia: That's not a 3( ). A tree or something could fall on your head.

Victor: Yeah, you're right. OK, let's 4( ). The storm can't last forever.

B. Choose the best answer.

1. ( ) Lydia is worried ________.
   A: the store may be closed
   B: the storm may last for days
   C: Victor could get hurt
   D: their pets are still outside

2. ( ) What is Victor probably going to do?
   A: Choose a movie to watch
   B: Finish eating his snacks
   C: Run to the convenience store
   D: Find his big umbrella

Discussion

Discuss these questions together.

1. How often are there typhoons in your area?
2. Do you remember any big typhoons?
3. What do you do during big storms?

18 Fast Food and Snacks

Part 1: Fast Food

Read the following article. Track 36

A lot of people love fast food. It tastes good. We can order and eat quickly. That saves time.

Fast food restaurants also sell toys. They are popular with children. Students like these restaurants, too. They meet friends there and study.

Be careful about eating too much fast food. It isn't good for you. Fortunately, hamburgers and french fries aren't the only menu items. Some fast food restaurants also sell healthy food like salad.

Vocabulary Check

Write the correct word in each blank.

taste	save	toy	healthy

1. What does it ____________ like? Is it salty?

2. Regular exercise helps you stay ____________.

3. ____________ your money. I'd like to pay this time.

4. That ____________ dog looks real. It even walks and barks.

Reading Check

Choose the best answer.

1. (　　) What is the problem with fast food?
   A: The restaurants have few tables.
   B: The prices are all too high.
   C: The food may be unhealthy.
   D: The restaurants don't sell salad.

2. (　　) Fast food is popular. Which of these reasons is not given?
   A: Ordering it takes little time.
   B: The restaurants sell toys.
   C: People like the taste.
   D: It has a lot of oil and salt.

3. (　　) "It isn't good for you." What is another way to say that?
   A: It's sold out.　　B: You think it's good.
   C: It isn't healthy.　　D: People don't eat it.

4. (　　) What does the article say about fast food restaurants?
   A: Most only sell hamburgers and french fries.
   B: Restaurants often change their menus.
   C: They may offer some healthy items.
   D: Salads at fast food restaurants are small.

Grammar Check

Write the correct word in each blank.

Ex: This donut is delicious. It's ___*also*___ really big!
(also / plus)

1. My brother likes that manga. I like it, ________.
   (too/plus)

2. Please get some eggs and milk. We ________ need bread.
   (more/also)

3. She loves chocolate cake ________ ice cream.
   (and/too)

4. This picture is nice. But that one is ________ colorful.
   (more/and)

Part 2: Coupons

Look at the following coupons.

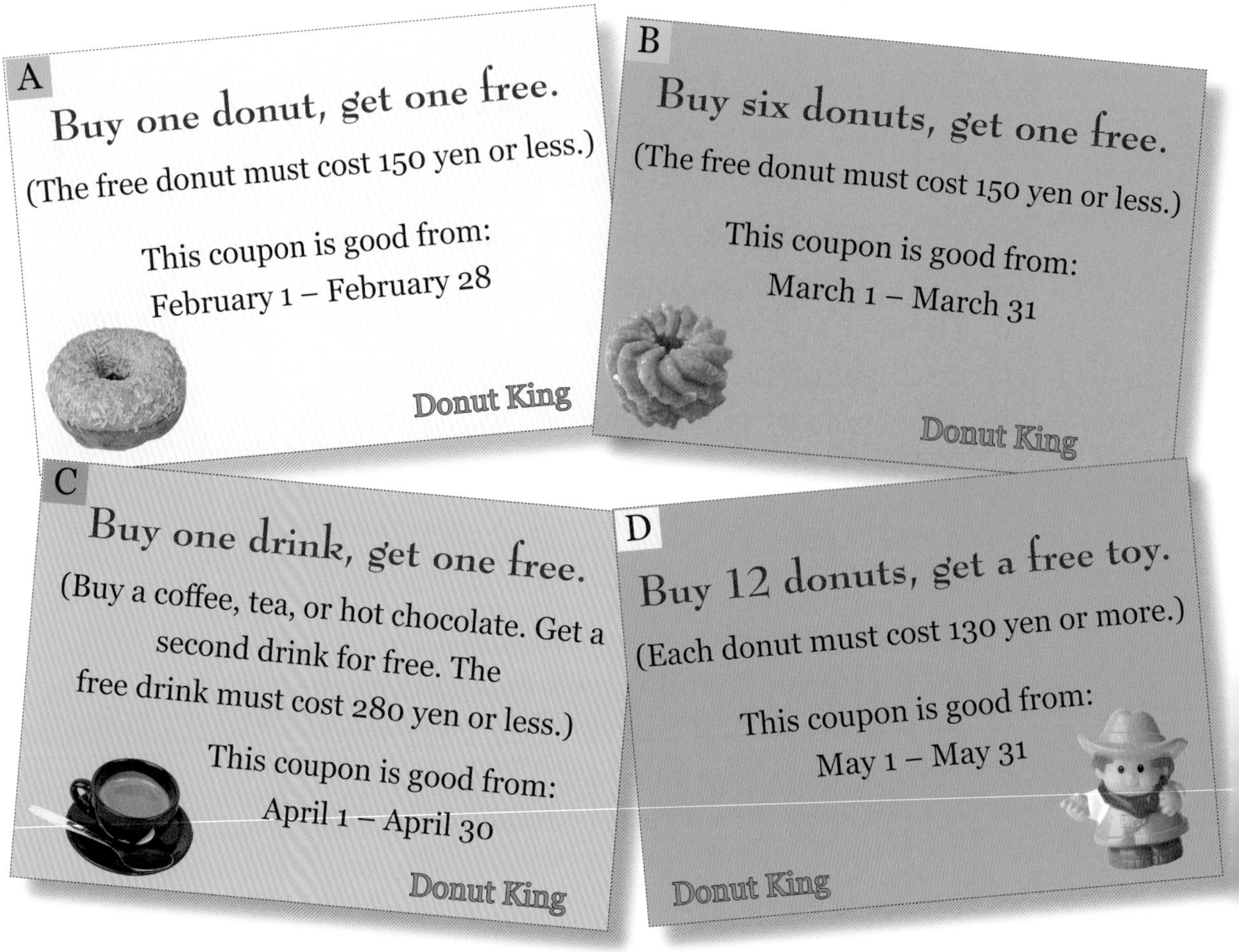

True or False

Circle true (T) or false (F).

1. (T/F) Every coupon offers a free item.
2. (T/F) Laura and her friend both want a coffee. They should use coupon C.
3. (T/F) You can get a toy with coupon B.
4. (T/F) The coupons are all good for one month.

Dictation

A. Listen and fill in the blanks. Track 37

Mark: Do you feel like a snack?

Rachel: Sure. There's an 1( ) shop near here. I think it's called Silver Scoop.

Mark: Silver Scoop is the best! But it's 2( ) on Mondays.

Rachel: Hmm...Marble Top has apple pie. Oh, 3( ). The owner is on vacation.

Mark: What else...Mindy's Place has 4( ). There's also Happy Beans.

Rachel: I like Happy Beans a lot. It's more of a coffee shop, though.

B. Choose the best answer.

1. ( ) Silver Scoop is a(n) __________.
   A: ice cream shop
   B: coffee shop
   C: pie maker
   D: supermarket

2. ( ) What is their best choice for a snack today?
   A: Marble Top B: Mindy's Place
   C: Silver Scoop D: Happy Beans

Discussion

Discuss these questions together.

1. Do you like fast food? If so, what restaurants do you go to?
2. What kinds of snacks do you like?
3. Do you have any favorite dessert shops or coffee shops?

19 Detectives

Part 1: An Interesting Line of Work

Read the following article. Track 38

Detectives have interesting jobs. They find out about people, companies, and so on. Then, they report on their findings.

A detective has to be smart. Finding information can be hard. The key is knowing where to look. Computers are a big help. Having good friends and contacts is also helpful.

Some detectives work for companies. Others work for the police. Some have their own offices. Their work is important. They help uncover the truth.

Vocabulary Check

Write the correct word in each blank.

information	office	interesting	report

1. I'm writing a book ____________. It's due next Monday.
2. Companies put so much ____________ on their websites.
3. My dad's ____________ is in that building. He works on the 5th floor.
4. It might be a(n) ____________ play. The writer is well-known.

Reading Check

Choose the best answer.

1. (   ) First, detectives find things out. Then, what do they do?
   A: They write reports.
   B: They call the police.
   C: They look for information.
   D: They get a job.

2. (   ) Which of these is true?
   A: All detectives work for the police.
   B: Few detectives are friendly.
   C: Most detectives have their own offices.
   D: Computers are helpful to detectives.

3. (   ) "They find out about people, companies, and so on." What does "and so on" mean?
   A: minus one
   B: and more
   C: on the way
   D: so-so

4. (   ) Why do detectives need good friends?
   A: To help them buy computers
   B: To help them uncover the truth
   C: To help them write reports
   D: To help them make new keys

Grammar Check

Complete each sentence with *about*, *for*, or *to*.

Ex: Is he making a new movie? What's it ___*about*___?

1. You can learn all __________ butterflies in that book.

2. This bowl is __________ holding fruit.

3. I mostly use my phone __________ send texts.

4. Are these shoes __________ hiking or running?

Part 2: Detective's Office

Read the following information.

Opening Hours

Monday – Friday:
9:30 AM – 12:00 PM
1:00 PM – 5:00 PM
6:00 PM – 8:00 PM

Saturday:
9:30 AM – 12:00 PM
1:00 PM – 6:00 PM

Sunday: 9:30 AM – 12:00 PM

Public Holidays: Closed

True or False

Circle true (T) or false (F).

1. (T/F) The office is open on Wednesday at 9:30 PM.

2. (T/F) On Friday afternoon, the office hours are 12:00 to 6:00.

3. (T/F) On Saturday, the detective takes a break at lunchtime.

4. (T/F) You can see the detective on Sundays.

Dictation

A. Listen and fill in the blanks. Track 39

Eileen: I'm looking for an 1(   ). Can you help me find him?

Fred: I'll do my best. Please write down his 2(   ). Does he live in Chicago?

Eileen: No, he's in another 3(   ) now – maybe New York.

Fred: I see. What kind of work does he do? Does he still have family here? Please write it all down.

Eileen: Of course. Could you use an old 4(   )?

Fred: Yes, thank you.

B. Choose the best answer.

1. (   ) Eileen's friend ________.
   A: might be in New York
   B: knows Fred well
   C: lives in Chicago
   D: hates taking photos

2. (   ) What doesn't Fred ask about?
   A: The person's birthday
   B: The person's job
   C: The person's family
   D: The person's name

Discussion

Discuss these questions together.

1. What would be interesting about being a detective?
2. Do you think detective work might be easy or hard?
3. Let's say you lose touch with a friend. How can you find him or her again?

20 Being Earth-Friendly

Part 1: Going Green

Read the following article. Track 40

We can all be Earth-friendly. Here are some ways to "go green."

Recycle your paper, cans, and bottles. Also, think about giving away your old things. It's better than throwing them away. Besides, other people may need them.

Turning on fewer lights saves electricity. Using less water is another great habit. So is using less plastic.

Try some of these ideas. Together, we can help the Earth smile again.

Vocabulary Check

Write the correct word(s) in each blank.

throw away	smile	idea	plastic

1. That's a good ____________. Everyone can bring food to the party.

2. Chika has such a pretty ____________. She should be a model.

3. Please don't ____________ that bottle. I want to put flowers in it.

4. The table is made of ____________. It's light and easy to carry.

Reading Check

Choose the best answer.

1. ( ) The article does not say we should recycle ___________.
   A: bottles B: paper
   C: lights D: cans

2. ( ) What should we do with old things?
   A: Throw them away.
   B: Don't do anything with them.
   C: Leave them outside.
   D: Give them to friends.

3. ( ) "Going green" means ___________.
   A: using more water
   B: buying many things
   C: choosing bright colors
   D: being Earth-friendly

4. ( ) Which of these people is going green?
   A: Robert: "I recycle cans and bottles."
   B: Jill: "I throw away my old clothes."
   C: Allen: "I leave the lights on all night."
   D: Charlene: "I wash my car every day."

Grammar Check

Write the correct word(s) in each blank.

Ex: I want to watch the video again. ___*It's*___ really funny.
(It's / There's)

1. Slow down. ____________________ no need to hurry.
   (There's/There are)

2. I love this weather. _____________ so warm and sunny.
   (There's/It's)

3. ____________________ three restaurants in the hotel.
   (There are/There's)

4. Don't worry about them. ____________________ coming later.
   (There are/They are)

Look at the following chart.

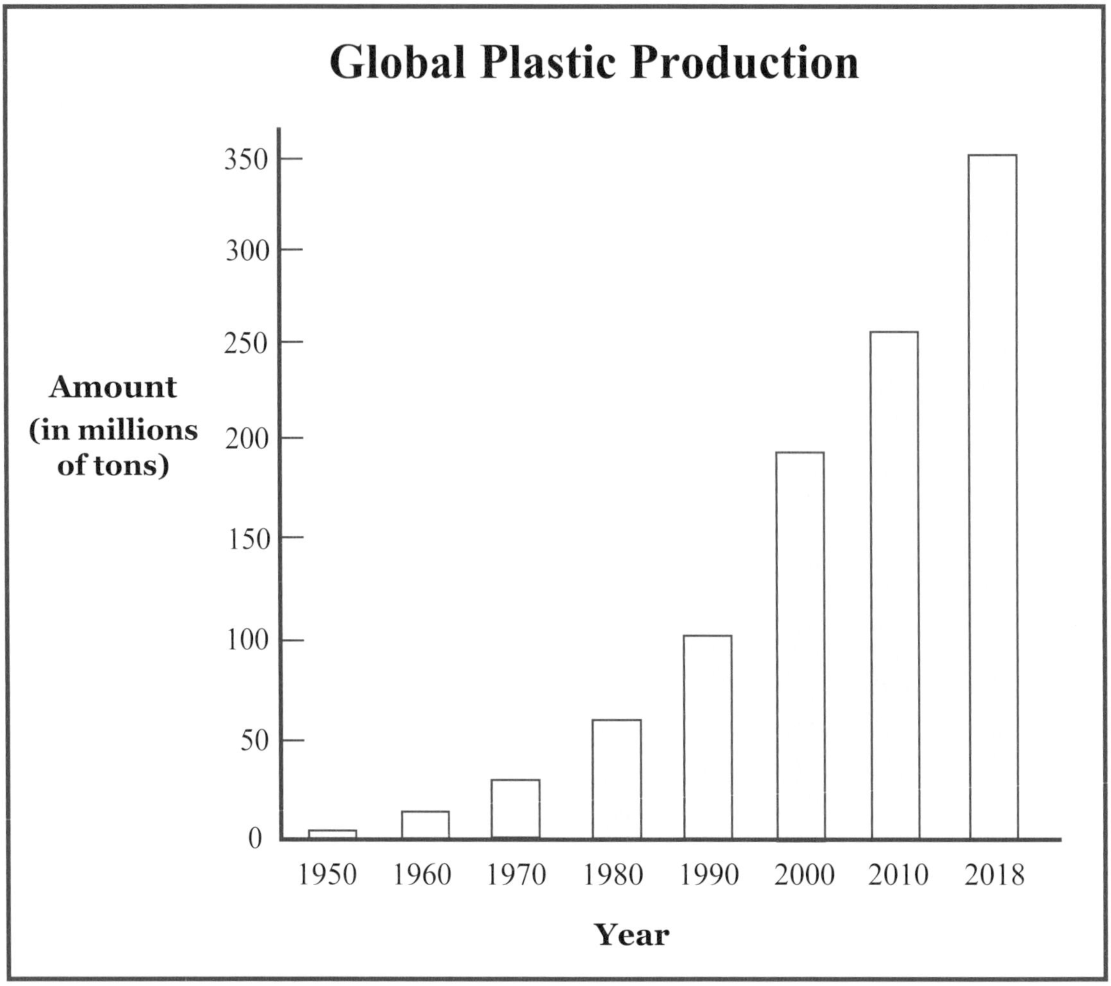

True or False

Circle true (T) or false (F).

1. (T/ F) We can see more than 60 years of data.

2. (T/ F) Every year, plastic production went up.

3. (T/ F) In 1990, plastic production was around 100 million tons.

4. (T/ F) The amount for 2010 was more than 300 million tons.

Dictation

A. Listen and fill in the blanks. Track 41

Ted: Hi, are you ready to go shopping?

Kumi: Almost. I just need to get my cloth $_1$( ).
I don't want to bring home more plastic bags.

Ted: I'm trying to use less plastic, too. I usually ask stores for $_2$( ) bags.

Kumi: I have an extra cloth one. Do you want to $_3$( )?

Ted: Sure, thanks. At least I have my blue water bottle.

Kumi: $_4$( )!

B. Choose the best answer.

1. ( ) Kumi shops with a ________ bag.
   A: cloth B: paper
   C: plastic D: blue

2. ( ) Which of these is true?
   A: Kumi has a bag for Ted to use.
   B: Both friends have a water bottle.
   C: Kumi asks stores for extra bags.
   D: Neither friend is shopping today.

Discussion

Discuss these questions together.

1. Plastic is in so many items. Is it easy or hard to use less plastic?
2. What are the best ways to "go green"?
3. How do you feel about the Earth's future? Can we solve our big problems?

Reading Links 1 [B-922]

リーディング・リンクス 1

1　刷　2021 年 1 月 18 日

2　刷　2024 年 3 月 29 日

著　者　アンドルー E. ベネット　Andrew E. Bennett

発行者　南雲　一範　Kazunori Nagumo
発行所　株式会社　南雲堂
〒162-0801　東京都新宿区山吹町 361
NAN' UN-DO CO.,Ltd.
361 Yamabuki-cho, Shinjuku-ku, Tokyo 162-0801, Japan
振替口座：00160-0-46863
TEL：03-3268-2311（代表）／ FAX：03-3269-2486
編集者　加藤 敦

製　版　Andrew E. Bennett

装　丁　銀月堂

検　印　省略

コード　ISBN 978-4-523-17922-1　C0082

Printed in Japan

E-mail　nanundo@post.email.ne.jp
URL　https://www.nanun-do.co.jp/